Adam and Eve
and the
Garden
of Eden

*I have dedicated this book to the children
of Shapla Primary School.*

The Eden Project brings plants and people together.
It is dedicated to developing a greater understanding
of our shared global garden; encouraging us to
respect plants and to protect them.

Adam and Eve and the Garden of Eden copyright © Random House U.K.
Copyright © Jane Ray, 2004

First published in Great Britain in 2004 by Random House U.K.
www.kidsatrandomhouse.co.uk

This edition published in 2005 under license from Random House U.K.
by Eerdmans Books for Young Readers,
an imprint of Wm. B. Eerdmans Publishing Co.
255 Jefferson SE, Grand Rapids, Michigan 49503
P.O. Box 163, Cambridge CB39PU U.K.

ISBN 0-8028-5278-5

05 06 07 08 09 10 11 9 8 7 6 5 4 3 2 1

Library of Congress Cataloging-in-Publication Data

Ray, Jane.
Adam and Eve and the Garden of Eden / written and illustrated by Jane Ray.-- 1st ed.
p. cm.
ISBN 0-8028-5278-5 (alk. paper)
1. Adam (Biblical figure)--Juvenile literature. 2. Eve (Biblical figure)--Juvenile literature. 3. Eden--Juvenile
literature. 4. Bible stories, English--O.T. Genesis. I. Title.
BSS580.A4R39 2005
222'.1109505--dc22
2004006804

Adam and Eve
and the
Garden
of Eden

Jane Ray

EERDMANS BOOKS FOR YOUNG READERS
GRAND RAPIDS, MICHIGAN / CAMBRIDGE, U.K.

At the very beginning of the world the earth was a dry and dusty place, where nothing could live and nothing could grow.

So God made a mist which watered the ground all over.

Then with his great hands, God formed the first man out of the clay of the newly watered earth.

God breathed the breath of life into the man's nostrils, so that he became a warm, living soul. God gave him a name, Adam, which means "earth."

In a place called Eden, God planted a garden for Adam. It was full of plants that were beautiful to look at and good to eat.

In the middle of the
garden stood a fountain.
Two great trees grew nearby,
the Tree of Knowledge and
the Tree of Life.

God warned Adam, "You may eat anything you like except the fruits from the Tree of Knowledge and the Tree of Life. If you eat them, you will die."

The Garden of Eden was beautiful.
The scent of blossoms filled the air.
Succulent fruits and berries
ripened in the sunshine.

Adam was happy to tend the
garden as God had asked him.

Adam loved his garden, but he was lonely. So God set about making creatures of every kind—the mighty and the meek, the sleek and the scaly, the spotted, feathered, dappled, and striped.

Some crept,
some slithered,
some hopped,
some swam,
some flew.
Adam named them, every one. But still he needed
a friend to share his home.

So God sent
Adam into a deep
and dreaming sleep.
While Adam dreamed,
God took out one of
his ribs and closed
him up again.
God turned the rib
into a woman, the
perfect partner for
Adam. She was called
Eve, which means
"mother of all
living things."

Now Adam and Eve looked after
their wonderful garden together.
They lived peacefully with
the animals.

They sang and they danced and they played—and sometimes they simply stood quietly and gazed at the beauty of it all. They never, ever tasted the fruit from the forbidden trees.

Then, one bright day, as Eve sat alone in
the shade of the Tree of Knowledge,
the serpent appeared beside her:

"I expect God told you not to eat the
fruit of this tree, hasn't he?" the serpent said.

Eve replied, "We can eat everything else,
but if we eat the fruit from this
tree, God says we'll die."

"Die? You won't die!"
The serpent crept closer
to Eve and whispered,
"The fruit from these
two trees will open
your eyes and make
you wise—like God.
Wouldn't you like that?"

The serpent melted away into the shadows,
and Eve was alone again. Eve looked at
the fruit of the Tree of Knowledge.
Would it really make her wise?

It smelled sweet.

Eve reached out her hand. The fruit was perfectly ripe.

Eve picked the fruit and bit into its juicy flesh.

When Adam came back, hot and thirsty, they ate the forbidden fruit together.

As soon as Adam and Eve
had eaten the fruit they looked
at each other, and for the first
time they felt shy.

They quickly found fig leaves
and covered themselves up.

Then they heard a voice calling them.
It was God, walking in the cool of the
garden. Adam and Eve felt ashamed and
hid from God in the bushes.

When God saw Adam and Eve
hiding, he knew that they
had done something wrong.
God told them to come out
from their hiding place.

God asked Adam, "Did you eat
the forbidden fruit?"
"I did," said Adam. "But it was
Eve who made me do it."
"Did you, Eve?" asked God.
"I did," said Eve. "But only because the
serpent persuaded me to."

God was very angry.

"Because of what you have done," God said to the serpent, "I am going to make you the most miserable creature on earth. You will slither everywhere on your belly, and you will eat nothing but dust."

God turned to Adam and Eve.
"Now you will learn what it is to be sad as well as
happy," God said. "You will work your fingers to the
bone growing food to eat and raising your children.
And when you die, you will return to the earth from
which you were made."

God loved Adam
and Eve as if they were his children,
but God knew that he must send them away
from the Garden of Eden.

"Leave, before you are tempted to eat
the fruit from the Tree of Life," God said.
"You are mortal now and cannot live
forever."

God gave Adam and Eve warm
clothes to wear. He handed them some
seeds and cuttings from the garden.
Then God sent them out into the world.

God commanded his angels
to guard the gates of Eden. By the
Tree of Life he set a bright flame, turning
this way and that, like a sword, to protect it.

In the bare earth beyond Eden, Adam and Eve planted a new garden for their family.